Jack's Garage:
Tire Maintenance for Kids

Written by **Jack Scudder**

Illustrated by **Nita Candra**

Scout & Company Publishing

For my dad, Trey

who taught me everything I know
about vehicle maintenance.

I love you.

Jack

For additional publications from Scout & Company, visit:

Did you know that tire service, especially correct tire pressure, is an important part of vehicle maintenance?

Your tires need air to function properly.

It's important to make sure
your tires have the proper
amount of air in them.

Ignoring tire pressure can cause uneven wear and imbalance, which can cause a blowout. The lower the pressure, the more dangerous it becomes.

With low air in the tires,
your truck also wouldn't
ride as smooth.

Do you know what fuel economy means? It is the amount of gas that you use when you travel a certain distance.

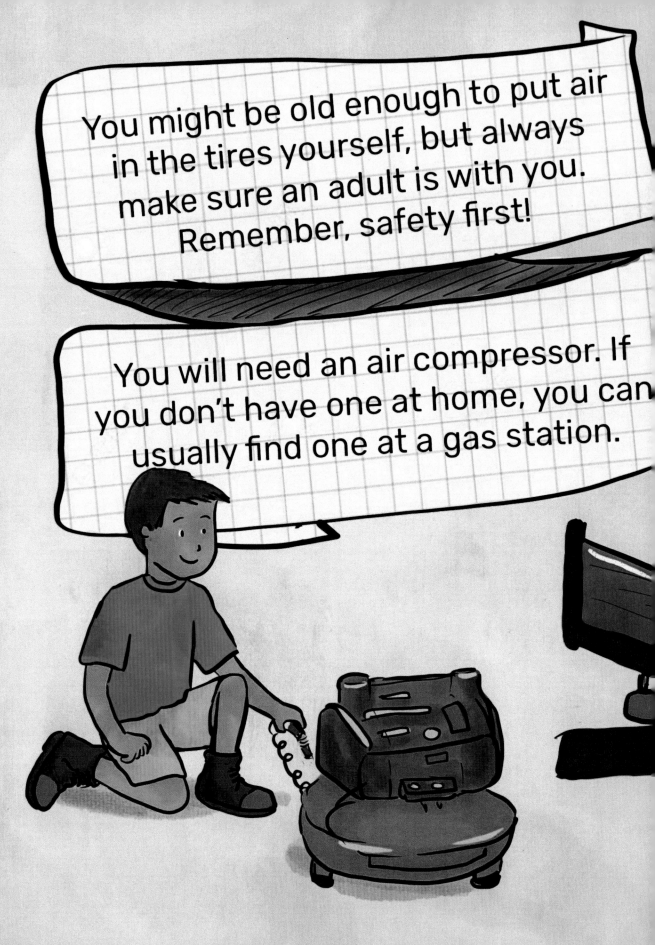

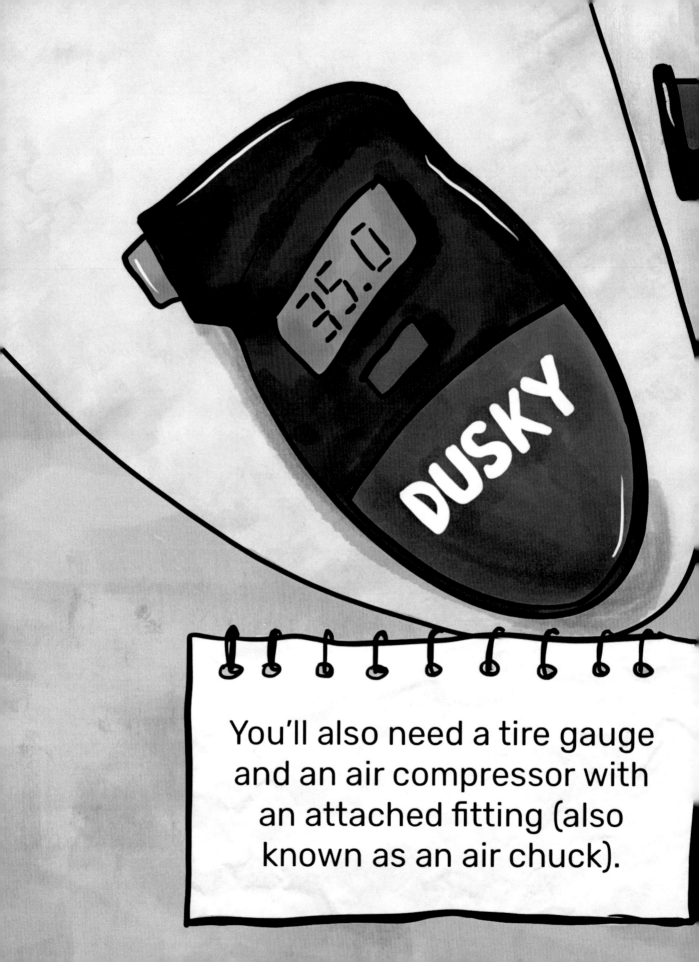

You'll also need a tire gauge and an air compressor with an attached fitting (also known as an air chuck).

Next, take off the valve stem caps.
Don't lose them!

How do you know if the tire pressure is right or wrong ? Look inside the door jam for the yellow sticker. It's on the driver's side. If you can't read it or if the tires aren't the originals, look on the sidewall of the tire itself.

Turn on the air compressor to fill the tire. Stop often to check the pressure with your tire gauge.

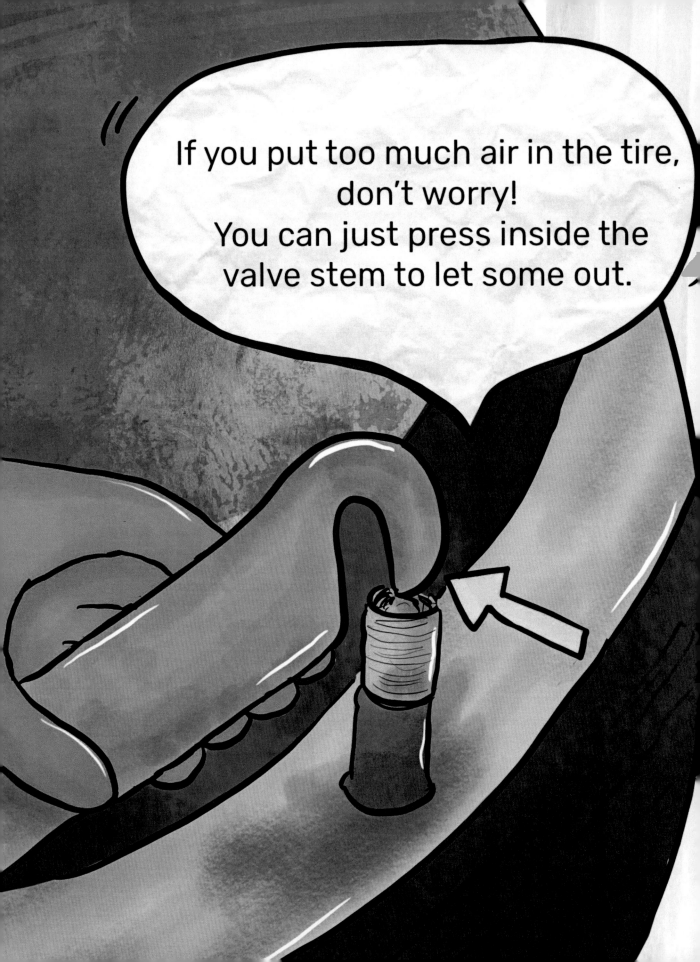

After filling all of your tires with air, inspect them one more time to make sure your valve stems are secure.

And now you're done!

Vocabulary:

Maintenance – the practice of taking care of something to keep it working properly

Tire pressure – the amount of air in a tire

Function – the purpose for which something exists

Wear – the condition of being worn down

Imbalance – out of balance; not balanced properly

Friction – the action of one surface or object rubbing against another

Air Compressor – a piece of equipment that presses air into a smaller space so that it can be used under high pressure

Tire Gauge – a tool that measures tire pressure

Valve Stem – a small tube on the tire that allows air to be added

Air Chuck – valve fittings that secure to a tire valve stem for tire pressure inflation and maintenance

Sidewall – the smooth, vertical area on the side of the tire between the edge of the tread and the bead of the tire

Inspect – to examine something to make sure that it meets a basic standard; to look something over

About the Author:

Jack is a first-time children's book author who wants to see more kids understand the inner workings of vehicles so that they know how to take care of them as they get older and start driving their own. Jack started working on vehicles alongside his dad when he was about 3 years old. Even if he was just holding a screwdriver off to the side, he was carefully observing and asking a bunch of questions. When Dad didn't know the answer, the two would sit side-by-side and look it up together. Once he mastered his first Radio Flyer tricycle, he moved on to scooters, motorcycles, tractors, cars, trucks (and even boats!). He's not afraid to get insanely dirty (much to Mom's chagrin) and knows more about carburetors than Crayola.

When Jack was old enough to start reading, he became obsessed with automotive shop manuals, *Chilton Repair Manuals* being his favorite. He'd pour through the contents like his friends obsessed over *Goosebumps*. He once found an old run-down Velo Solex motorized bike on the curb, pushed it home to inspect, then insisted that mom print the entire manual from the internet so he can break down the engine part-by-painstaking-part until he finally figured out the problem. He knows his old Craftsman tractor like the back of his hand. And, by the time Jack was 10 years old, he had his heart set on buying a fixer-upper truck to work on with his dad. At 12 years old, that's exactly what he did. And he can't even legally drive it yet.

Jack lives in Florida with his family. He's a military kid and proud of it! Mom is retired U.S. Air Force, a 15-year classroom teacher, and an award-winning children's book author. Dad is a Captain in the U.S. Navy. Jack started homeschooling in 5th grade, loves the flexibility of his schedule, and stays busy with his local Sea Cadets unit on many weekends. When he's not tinkering in the garage, he's SCUBA diving, tearing apart and rebuilding computers, gaming, and generally driving his mother crazy.

Resources:

For study guides and additional resources, as well as special bonuses,

please visit www.facebook.com/scoutandcompanypublishing/

and

www.Victoria-Scudder.com

This book belongs to:

_____

30785619R00018